Lincolnwood Library
4000 W. Pratt Ave.
Lincolnwood, IL 60712

GREAT MINDS OF SCIENCE

STEPHEN
HAWKING
Extraordinary Theoretical Physicist

by Karen Latchana Kenney

Content Consultant
Scott Watson
Assistant Physics Professor
Syracuse University

Core Library

An Imprint of Abdo Publishing
www.abdopublishing.com

www.abdopublishing.com

Published by Abdo Publishing, a division of ABDO, PO Box 398166,
Minneapolis, Minnesota 55439. Copyright © 2015 by Abdo Consulting
Group, Inc. International copyrights reserved in all countries. No part of this
book may be reproduced in any form without written permission from the
publisher. Core Library™ is a trademark and logo of Abdo Publishing.

Printed in the United States of America, North Mankato, Minnesota
042014
092014

Cover Photo: Gareth Fuller/PA Wire/AP Images
Interior Photos: Gareth Fuller/PA Wire/AP Images, 1; Rex Features/AP
Images, 4, 32, 45; Ron Ellis/Shutterstock Images, 7; JeniFoto/Shutterstock
Images, 9; Lionel Cironneau/AP Images, 12; Banderlog/Shutterstock Images,
15; Ted S. Warren/AP Images, 20; Red Line Editorial, 25; The Royal Society/
NASA, 26; David Banks/AP Images, 30; Loen Neal/AFP/Getty Images/
Newscom, 34, 43; Lynne Sladky/AP Images, 36; Jim Campbell/Aero-News
Network/NASA, 39; Paul Alers/NASA, 40

Editor: Jenna Gleisner
Series Designer: Becky Daum

Library of Congress Control Number: 2014932696

Cataloging-in-Publication Data
Kenney, Karen Latchana.
 Stephen Hawking: extraordinary theoretical physicist / Karen Latchana
Kenney.
   p. cm. -- (Great minds of science)
Includes bibliographical references and index.
ISBN 978-1-62403-381-0
1. Hawking, Stephen, 1942- --Juvenile literature. 2. Physicists--Great Britain-
-Biography--Juvenile literature. 3. Scientists--Great Britain--Biography--
Juvenile literature. 4. Black holes (Astronomy)--Juvenile literature. I. Title.
530.092--dc23
[B]
                                                          2014932696

CONTENTS

CHAPTER ONE

ASKING THE BIG QUESTIONS

Where did we come from? Did the universe have a beginning? If so, how will it end? Even as a young teenager, these were the big questions Stephen Hawking thought about. Stephen and his friends discussed their ideas. Was the universe growing or standing still? This future scientist would spend his life's work trying to find the answers to these questions.

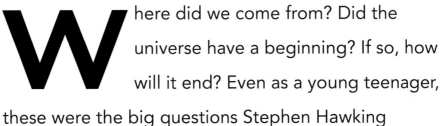

Stephen Hawking is one of the most famous theoretical physicists.

Galileo Galilei

Stephen Hawking likes to tell others that he was born exactly 300 years after Galileo Galilei's death. Galileo was an important Italian astronomer born in 1564. His work changed human knowledge about motion and astronomy. He improved the telescope, a new instrument at the time. Galileo used his powerful telescopes to observe the stars and planets. He recorded the phases of Earth's moon. He also discovered four moons orbiting Jupiter. Throughout his life, Galileo studied the stars and planets. He became known as the father of modern science. Galileo's discoveries changed how scientists study the universe and inspired Stephen.

A Different Family

Stephen Hawking was born in Oxford, England, on January 8, 1942. His father, Frank, was a medical research scientist. His mother, Isobel, was a graduate from Oxford University. She stayed home with Stephen and his three siblings: Mary, Philippa, and Edward. Stephen's family was very unusual and intelligent. They loved books and even read them while eating dinner. They also talked very fast. To talk

In his first year at Saint Albans School, a combined middle and high school just north of London, 11-year-old Stephen ranked close to the bottom of the class.

even faster, they made up their own language. Others called it *Hawkingnese*.

Creating and Building

Although he was smart, Stephen was not a great student. But other students at his school, Saint Albans

School, noticed Stephen's intelligence. They nicknamed him "Einstein." Stephen had a close group of friends. They created complex board games and built fireworks together. The group also built a computer out of recycled clock and machine parts. They called it LUCE. This computer could solve simple math problems. At age 14 Stephen decided to focus on math and physics. At his father's advice, Stephen also studied chemistry. He later applied to Oxford University in the United Kingdom. He was accepted as a student when he was only 17 years old.

Board Games

One game Stephen and his friends created was a game about manufacturing called Risk. It included railways, factories, and a stock market. The game took days to complete. Another was a war game. Its game board had 4,000 squares. A social and political game based on medieval England was equally complicated. Each player was a dynasty that had a complex family tree.

As had happened at Saint Albans, Stephen was not very involved in his schoolwork at Oxford University.

College Life

In 1960 Stephen began his first year at Oxford. He majored in natural sciences, a course of study that includes biology, chemistry, and other sciences that help us better understand how the natural world works. Stephen could not focus on a math major because the school did not offer this course of study.

In his third and final year at Oxford, Stephen began having some physical problems. He fell down a flight of stairs. He was getting clumsy. But Stephen was not sure what was causing the problems. He would find out while at Cambridge University in England. This is where he began his research of the stars and the origins of the universe.

In his autobiography *My Brief History*, Stephen Hawking recalls his early thoughts and questions about the universe:

> *I had six or seven close friends, most of whom I'm still in touch with. We used to have long discussions and arguments about everything from radio-controlled models to religion. . . . One of the things we talked about was the origin of the universe and whether it had required a God to create it and set it going. I had heard that light from distant galaxies was shifted toward the red end of the [light] spectrum and that this was supposed to indicate that the universe was expanding. . . . I was sure there must be some other reason for the red shift. An essentially unchanging and everlasting universe seemed so much more natural. Maybe light just got tired, and more red, on its way to us, I speculated.*

Source: Stephen Hawking. My Brief History. New York: Bantam Books, 2013. Print. 25–26.

Changing Minds

This passage discusses what Stephen talked about with his friends when he was young. Think about what one of his friends might have to say about the same discussions. Write a paragraph that expresses that point of view. How might the friend have felt about talking with Stephen about the universe? What might have he said about its origins?

CHAPTER TWO

A REASON TO WORK

Hawking really began to study the universe at Cambridge while working toward a more advanced degree. He entered the field of cosmology. This is the study of the origin and growth of the universe. Most of this type of work can only be done through developing theories. These theories are difficult to test and prove because the universe is an immense place and cannot

Jane Wilde, Hawking's first wife, inspired him to keep working after he was diagnosed with amyotrophic lateral sclerosis (ALS).

be completely explored or understood by humans. Hawking also decided to focus on general relativity. This is one of famous physicist Albert Einstein's theories. General relativity explains how gravity and time work and how objects move. Einstein showed that space and time are connected. This connection is called space-time. Einstein's theory showed that large objects, such as planets, bend the space-time around them. This bend in space-time pulls on other objects. This pull is a planet's force of gravity. It is what keeps a moon in a planet's orbit.

Studying the Big Bang Theory

Cosmology was a popular area of research in the 1920s and 1930s. Even Einstein had questioned whether or not the universe expanded. Hawking was drawn to the possibilities of the universe. The big question in cosmology was whether the universe had a starting point or not. Many believed that it did not and instead new matter appeared as galaxies spread

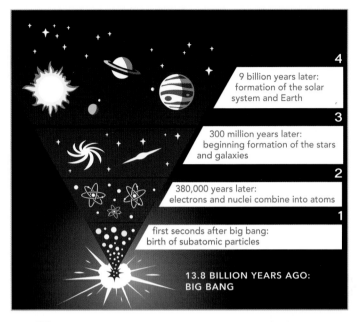

Big Bang Theory
This diagram shows the theory of how the universe expanded from a single point. After reading about the big bang theory, what did you think the universe's growth looked like? What does this diagram tell you that the text did not? Does the diagram help you better understand this theory?

apart. This was known as the steady state theory. But a newer theory challenged that thought.

The big crunch theory proposed that the universe would grow to a maximum size and then collapse. Hawking wondered about a big bang theory: If the universe could end at a single point, perhaps it also started at a single point. Maybe it then expanded out from that point. As it grew over billions of years, galaxies, planets, and stars formed. The question about a singular universal starting point intrigued Hawking. This big bang theory later became a focus of his research.

More Physical Problems

During his first year at Cambridge, Hawking's physical problems got worse. He couldn't tie his shoes. His speech was slurred. It was harder and harder for others to understand what he said. When he went home for Christmas, his parents noticed the changes in Hawking's physical abilities. Hawking went ice-skating and fell. He was not able to get up. His mother convinced Hawking to see a doctor. After many doctor visits and tests, Hawking learned the shocking news. He had amyotrophic lateral sclerosis, or ALS, a rare disease that could not be cured. He was told he would probably live just two to three more years. Hawking was only 21 years old.

Working and Living for Jane

Around the time of his diagnosis, Hawking met Jane Wilde at a New Year's party in January 1963. She was finishing high school and about to start studying at Westfield College. It was the beginning of a romance. But Hawking was also depressed about the news of his illness. He wasn't sure if he should continue his research. He felt lost.

What Is ALS?

Amyotrophic lateral sclerosis is a disease that attacks nerve cells in the brain and spine. The first signs are slurred speech and weakness and twitching in the hands. Swallowing becomes difficult. Eventually most muscles stop working and patients cannot move or speak. The disease does not affect muscles such as the heart or lungs, and it also does not affect the brain. So people with ALS still have the function of their vital organs. Their minds also work perfectly well.

Eventually Hawking realized that he wanted to make the best of his time left. He continued working.

Two years after his diagnosis, Hawking was still alive despite predictions that he would not survive. In

"Properties of Expanding Universes"

In 1965 scientists discovered radiation coming from outside our galaxy. It showed that the universe had once been very hot. This supported the big bang theory. That same year, Hawking finished a paper titled "Properties of Expanding Universes." In it he presented his ideas about the universe beginning at a single point. He also discussed the properties of a universe that began with a big bang, such as the presence of microwave radiation. It showed that the universe may have had a hot and explosive beginning.

fact, the disease seemed to be slowing. Hawking and Jane soon became engaged and were later married in 1965. Jane gave Hawking something to live for. He was driven to finish his college degree and get a job. He wanted to be working before he was married.

The physicist dove into his research with full force. He applied for a research fellowship and was granted one at Caius College in Cambridge. He wrote an essay titled "Singularities and the Geometry of Space-Time." The essay won a famous science award—the Adams Prize.

It brought Hawking great recognition in his field. He was being noticed as a young scientist with a very promising future. Hawking was working and enjoying it unlike ever before. He was now ready to find some answers to his questions about the universe.

FURTHER EVIDENCE

Chapter Two mentions Albert Einstein and his theory of general relativity. What does the chapter tell you about his theories about space? Check out the website below. Does the information on this website support the explanation of theories in this chapter? Write a few sentences using new information from the website as evidence to support the theory's explanation in this chapter.

Changing Theories
www.mycorelibrary.com/stephen-hawking

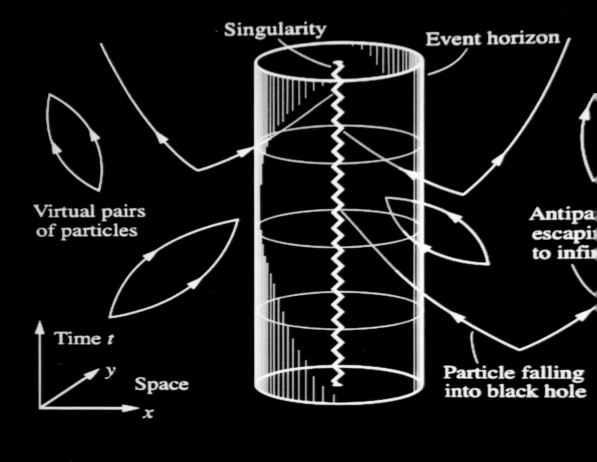

Singularity   Event horizon

Virtual pairs
of particles

Antipa
escapi
to infi

Time *t*

y

Space

x

Particle falling
into black hole

CHAPTER THREE

INTO BLACK HOLES

While Hawking focused on his work, his disease gradually became worse. By 1969 he was confined to a wheelchair. ALS slowed him down physically. But it did not hold back his career. Hawking worked on the theory of how the universe began and was expanding. In 1970 he realized a way to study the universe's beginning. Black holes were the key. Black holes are mysterious, dark

Hawking lectures about black holes at the Seattle Science Festival Luminaries Series in 2012.

places in space. Gravity is very strong in these places. Matter that gets too close is squeezed into the center of a black hole. Scientists believe many black holes form when stars die. The star collapses into a dense point—the center of a black hole. Some black holes are tiny. Others are huge.

Fatherhood

In 1967 Hawking had his first child, Robert. His daughter, Lucy, was born in 1969. His third child, Tim, was born in 1979. Because of his disability, Hawking could not help much with his children. His wife, Jane, had to physically care for them.

Studying Black Holes

Scientists can study black holes by looking at their edges. That is where light and gases can be seen. The edge of a black hole is called the event horizon. Particles inside a black hole would have to move faster than the speed of light to escape it. But nothing can move faster than light. Light cannot escape, making a black hole dark. Hawking realized that black holes could never become smaller. They could only grow larger. This is because nothing inside a black hole can escape its gravity. But then Hawking thought about the particles at the event horizon. What happened to those particles?

Hawking Radiation

Hawking shifted his focus. To understand the large universe, the physicist looked at some of the smallest particles. Pairs of particles exist and constantly appear in space. One part of the pair has a negative charge. The other part has a positive charge. The particles stay together for a period of time and then separate. After separating they later collide and destroy each other. Hawking believed that many of these particle

---

The Speed of Light

Light particles travel from one point to the next. The light we see comes from a source, such as the sun. It takes time for light to travel a distance from its source to our eyes. It takes roughly eight minutes for light from the sun to reach Earth. Light moves incredibly fast. Nothing can travel faster than light. Its speed is 186,282 miles per second (299,792 km per second).

pairs existed at a black hole's event horizon. When they separate, the negative particle goes into the black hole. The positive particle can then escape. This meant that black holes emitted energy. This energy became known as Hawking radiation.

A Scientific Breakthrough

Hawking radiation was a scientific breakthrough. It showed that positive particles could escape the edges of black holes. But the negative particles fell into a black hole. They slowly shrank the black hole's center. This proved that a black hole could actually get smaller. As it collapsed, the center would eventually explode. Matter would then fly out into space.

Hawking tested his theory. He went over his equations. It was such a new and radical idea. He wanted to be sure he was correct before announcing it to the scientific world. He first showed his equations to friends and colleagues. Some agreed, but others didn't. Hawking published his theory in 1974 in his paper "Black Hole Explosions?" At first other

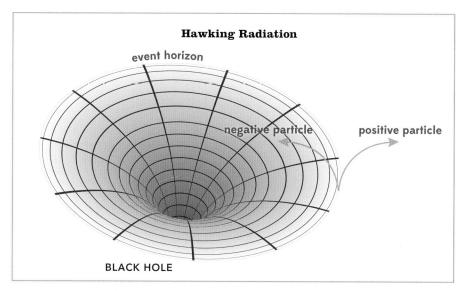

Hawking Radiation

This diagram shows how positive particles escape black holes. After reading about Hawking radiation, what did you think a black hole looked like? What does this diagram tell you that the text did not? Does the diagram help you better understand how particles act near black holes?

scientists thought his idea was nonsense. But by 1976 most scientists had come to accept Hawking's theory. The discovery of Hawking radiation forever changed the study of black holes. The mathematics Hawking used to understand black holes has helped us understand the beginning of the universe. Using his equations, Hawking was able to show that the universe must have begun at a single point.

CHAPTER FOUR

BECOMING FAMOUS

In 1974 Hawking had been elected to become a member of the Royal Society. This group was founded in the 1660s. Its members are some of the most important scientists in the world. In 1975 Pope Paul VI recognized Hawking for his work on the big bang theory. Hawking was awarded the Pius XI Medal. He also won the Albert Einstein Award, a US award given to physicists, in 1978. And in 1979

In 2006 the Royal Society awarded Hawking the Copley Medal, the oldest award for scientific achievement, for his contributions to theoretical physics and cosmology.

Hawking became the seventeenth Lucasian Professor of Mathematics at the University of Cambridge. Famous physicist Sir Isaac Newton held this honored position from 1669 to 1702. Hawking signed his name in a university record after accepting this position. It was the last time he was able to do so.

Sir Isaac Newton

Born in 1643, Isaac Newton was one of the greatest minds in physics. His book *Philosophiae Naturalis Principia Mathematica* (Mathematical Principles of Natural Philosophy) showed how gravity worked on all objects in the universe. Newton also worked with light and optics. He invented a new and better kind of telescope. Its basic design is still used today. Newton was the second Lucasian Professor and was knighted in 1705.

Losing the Ability to Speak

Hawking's health was getting worse. It was more and more difficult for others to understand Hawking's speech. Only a few people understood him, including his secretary. She typed out his scientific papers. An interpreter translated his seminars to students.

He had long choking fits and almost died while visiting Sweden in 1985. He was rushed back to Cambridge, where doctors performed surgery to help Hawking breathe. Hawking survived, but the surgery took away his ability to speak. He also now needed nursing care day and night.

Hawking's voice was silent, but his mind was still active. He was mostly paralyzed, but he could move parts of his face and hands. A computer expert in California heard of Hawking's loss of speech. He sent Hawking a computer program to help him speak.

Spelling Cards

Before Hawking received his computerized voice, he had to use a spelling card to communicate. Someone held up a card with the alphabet on it and pointed one-by-one to the letters. When the person pointed to the letter Hawking wanted to use, he raised his eyebrow. This was repeated over and over until a word or a sentence was spelled out. It worked, but it was an incredibly slow and frustrating process. It was nearly impossible to have a conversation or write a science paper using the spelling card system.

Hawking's computer program and voice synthesizer has helped him give lectures and presentations around the world.

The computer program showed a series of screens with words. Hawking used a hand controller to select words. The sentences he built were then sent to a machine that spoke the words. This system gave Hawking the ability to communicate again. It also made it much easier for others to understand him. He gave speeches and ended up writing seven books using different forms of the system.

Writing Science for Everyone

One of Hawking's books made him famous around the world. He wanted to write a book about the universe that every person could understand. He decided to avoid using math equations. Instead he used humor and analogies to help readers understand complex ideas. His book *A Brief History of Time* was published in 1988. It was an immediate success. The book was on the *New York Times* bestseller list for 147 weeks. Hawking was now famous—a sort of science superstar.

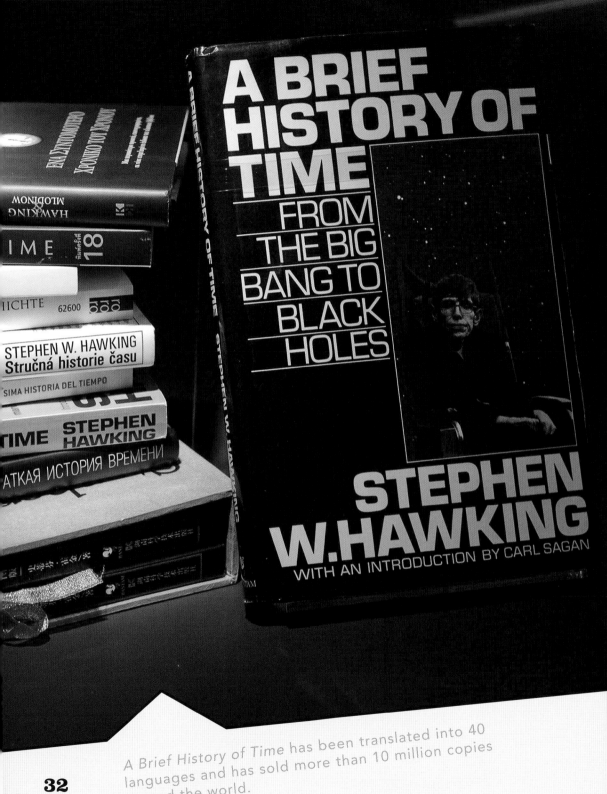

A Brief History of Time has been translated into 40 languages and has sold more than 10 million copies around the world.

Stephen Hawking's book *A Brief History of Time* brought complex ideas about the universe to everyday people. In this excerpt, Hawking describes how he first started thinking about particles at the edges of black holes:

> *Before 1970, my research on general relativity had concentrated mainly on the question of whether or not there had been a big bang singularity. However, one evening in November that year . . . I started to think about black holes as I was getting into bed. My disability makes this a rather slow process, so I had plenty of time. At that date there was no precise definition of which points in space-time lay in a black hole and which lay outside. . . . The boundary of the black hole, the event horizon, is formed by the light rays that just fail to escape from the black hole, hovering forever just on the edge. It is a bit like running away from the police and just managing to keep one step ahead but not being able to get clear away!*

> Source: Stephen Hawking. *A Brief History of Time.* New York: Bantam Books, 1996. Print. 103.

What's the Big Idea?

Take a close look at this excerpt. What is Hawking trying to say about particles around black holes? Pick out two details he uses to make his point. What analogy does he use to describe the particles?

CHAPTER FIVE

MOVING TOWARD THE FUTURE

After publishing his bestselling book, Hawking stayed busy thinking, writing, traveling, and working. He was featured in magazines around the world. He inspired others to achieve their goals in spite of tragedy or disability. His home life began to suffer though. In 1990 he left his wife for his nurse, Elaine Mason. Hawking and Mason

Hawking joined in the opening ceremony of the 2012 Paralympic Games in London.

Although Mason was once Hawking's nurse, their marriage did not last long.

were married in 1995 and had a stormy relationship. In 2006 they both filed for divorce.

Time Traveling in Space?

Hawking's mind continued to wander to different ideas. He began thinking and lecturing about the possibility of time travel. Some scientists thought it might be possible to time travel in space through wormholes. Wormholes are tubes through space-time. They could possibly connect distant places in space. Going through one might be similar to traveling to a faraway place in only an instant of time. Hawking thought that if wormholes existed, baby universes might be at the other ends of the tubes. Those universes might connect to other universes. Traveling through one might never be possible. But Hawking thinks it is an interesting idea for scientists to ponder.

Hawking hopes to travel into space himself. He might get the chance. Hawking is scheduled to fly on billionaire

A TV Star

As Hawking's fame grew, he was asked to appear on popular television shows. He appeared on *The Simpsons*, *Star Trek*, *Late Night with Conan O'Brien*, and *The Big Bang Theory*. In *The Simpsons*, Hawking tells main character Homer that his theory of a donut-shaped universe was interesting. He told Homer he might even steal it! The show's producers made an action figure of Hawking. It sold out in many toy stores.

Zero Gravity

Peter Diamandis is the founder of the X Prize Foundation, which offers cash prizes to inventors who can solve big challenges. He runs a company that lets people experience weightlessness and train as if they were astronauts at NASA's Kennedy Space Center in Florida. He offered this opportunity to Hawking, who immediately agreed. In 2007 Hawking had his chance. He floated free of his wheelchair in weightlessness. It was the closest thing available to being in space. Hawking found it to be an amazing experience.

businessman Richard Branson's *Virgin Galactic* spaceship. This spaceship will allow commercial passengers to travel into space. Its first flight was expected to happen in 2014, although in 2013 the aircraft was still being tested. Hawking, actor Leonardo DiCaprio, and nearly 700 other people have signed up to fly on Branson's spacecraft. The spacecraft will fly to the upper edge of the atmosphere, where passengers can experience weightlessness. Hawking's dream of space travel may come true.

Hawking enjoyed zero gravity at NASA's Kennedy Space Center in 2007.

Speaking Up about Climate Change

Now in his 70s, Hawking uses his celebrity status to talk to the public about global disasters. A disaster, such as global warming, could eventually make it impossible for humans to live on the planet. Hawking believes that humans need to find a way to travel long distances in space. In his opinion, it is important for humans to live in space or find another planet to live

Hawking is praised by his daughter, Lucy, during his presentation titled "Why We Should Go into Space" at NASA's fiftieth anniversary in 2008.

on. This may save the human race from disappearing. Hawking believes humans need to do so in the next 100 years.

Hawking's Legacy

The questions Hawking has asked have opened up new worlds of thought in science. The study of black holes has been forever changed. And our understanding of the universe has grown. Hawking's disability never slowed his mind down. He used what he could use—his mind—to the best of his ability. His life has been full and rich with accomplishment. And his ideas have touched millions of others around the world. Hawking still imagines possibilities. His theories continue to challenge our knowledge of the world and the universe.

EXPLORE ONLINE

Chapter Five focuses on Hawking's thoughts about time travel and space flight. It also touches on wormholes. The website below focuses on the possibility of wormhole voyages. As you know, every source is different. How is the information given in the website different from the information in this chapter? What information is the same? How do the two sources present information differently? What can you learn from this website?

Wormhole Voyages

www.mycorelibrary.com/stephen-hawking

Black Holes and Hawking Radiation

Hawking's discoveries about black holes changed what scientists believed about our universe's history. Hawking proved that a black hole could actually get smaller. Because of Hawking's work, scientists now know that black holes are not places in space where objects, such as light and stars, only disappear.

The Big Bang Theory

Hawking used his discoveries about black holes to study the big bang theory. This is the idea that the universe began at a singular starting point. Hawking showed that as a black hole collapsed, the center would eventually explode. Matter would then fly out into space. Black holes could then be beginning points in space. This supported the theory that the universe began at a single point. Hawking's research has helped scientists understand more about the nature and origin of the universe.

A Brief History of Time

Hawking wanted to share his ideas about the universe's origins with everyday people not involved in scientific study. He wrote his book *A Brief History of Time* in 1988. He used humor and analogies to help explain physics and cosmology to readers. His book became a bestseller and made him famous. Because of Hawking's book, many readers have a better understanding of the universe, black holes, and the big bang theory.

STOP AND THINK

Say What?

Studying about the universe and black holes can mean learning a lot of new vocabulary. Find five words in this book that you have never seen or heard before. Use a dictionary to find out what they mean. Then write the meanings in your own words, and use each word in a new sentence.

Why Do I Care?

Black holes exist far away from Earth in space. Although you may never travel to any black holes, their effects can help us understand the universe. Why do you think it is important to understand black holes? Does knowing about the universe change your life? If so, how?

Surprise Me

Chapter Three discusses black holes. After reading this book, what two or three facts about black holes did you find most surprising? Write a few sentences about each fact. Why did you find them surprising?

You Are There

This book discusses when Hawking learned about his disability. Imagine that you are a scientist who has learned that you have a health problem or disease that will drastically change your life. How do you feel about the news? What do you think about continuing your scientific work?

GLOSSARY

astronomy
the study of the stars, planets, and space

breakthrough
an important step taken toward understanding or knowing about something

cosmology
the science of the origin and growth of the universe

galaxy
a large grouping of stars and planets in space

global warming
the gradual rise of Earth's temperature caused by man-made gases trapped in Earth's atmosphere

gravity
the force responsible for giving weight to matter and causing all objects to attract to one another

matter
anything that has weight and takes up space

physics
the science that focuses on matter and energy, including the study of light, sound, heat, motion, electricity, and force

radiation
the sending out of rays of heat, light, or other type of energy

universe
everything that exists in space, including black holes, stars, and planets

LEARN MORE

Books

Aguilar, David A. *Space Encyclopedia: A Tour of Our Solar System and Beyond.* Washington, DC: National Geographic, 2013.

Canavan, Thomas. *Why Are Black Holes Black? Questions and Answers About Space.* Mankato, MN: Arcturus, 2014.

Fleisher, Paul. *The Big Bang.* Minneapolis, MN: Twenty-First Century Books, 2006.

Websites

To learn more about Great Minds of Science, visit **booklinks.abdopublishing.com**. These links are routinely monitored and updated to provide the most current information available.

Visit **www.mycorelibrary.com** for free additional tools for teachers and students.

INDEX

ABOUT THE AUTHOR

Karen Latchana Kenney is a Minneapolis author and editor who has written more than 80 books. Science is one of her favorite topics to write about, and Stephen Hawking is one of her personal heroes.